Where Does the Bathwater Go?

By Daisy Allyn

Gareth Stevens
Publishing

Please visit our website, www.garethstevens.com. For a free color catalog of all our high-quality books, call toll free 1-800-542-2595 or fax 1-877-542-2596.

Library of Congress Cataloging-in-Publication Data

Allyn, Daisy.
Where does the bathwater go? / Daisy Allyn.
    p. cm. — (Everyday mysteries)
Includes index.
ISBN 978-1-4339-6323-0 (pbk.)
ISBN 978-1-4339-6324-7 (6-pack)
ISBN 978-1-4339-6321-6 (library binding)
1. Water-supply—Juvenile literature. I. Title.
TD348.A56 2012
628.3—dc23

                                    2011021348

First Edition

Published in 2012 by
Gareth Stevens Publishing
111 East 14th Street, Suite 349
New York, NY 10003

Copyright © 2012 Gareth Stevens Publishing

Designer: Katelyn E. Reynolds
Editor: Greg Roza

Photo credits: Cover, pp. 1, 5 (inset), 7, 9, 11 (both), 17, 19, (pp. 3–24 background and graphics) Shutterstock.com; p. 5 (main image) Lauren Burke/Stone/Getty Images; pp. 13, 15 (inset) iStockphoto.com; p. 15 (main image) iStockphoto/Thinkstock.

Printed in the United States of America

CPSIA compliance information: Batch #CW12GS: For further information contact Gareth Stevens, New York, New York at 1-800-542-2595.

Contents

Boldface words appear in the glossary.

Water in Our Homes

People who have running water in their homes use it for many things. They drink it, cook with it, and wash with it. Have you ever wondered what happens to this water when it goes down the **drain**? Let's find out!

drain

5

Moving Water

Water moves down the drain because of **gravity**. Sometimes people need water to move up. Then they use tools called pumps to bring water into their homes. There are many kinds of pumps.

Well Water

In the country, some people have wells. A well is a hole in the ground that's deep enough to reach water. People once used a pail and rope to bring well water up. Today, most people pump well water into their homes.

Stored Water

In towns and cities where many people live, water is stored in lakes and water towers. Some places store water in man-made lakes called reservoirs (REH-zuh-vwahrz). The water is pumped into homes and businesses.

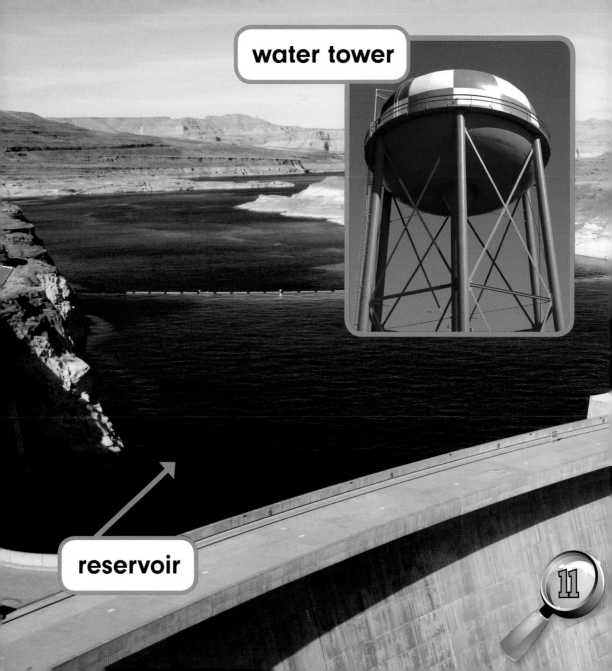

water tower

reservoir

11

What's a Septic System?

In some places, wastewater leaves a home and enters an underground **tank**. This is called a septic tank. There, **bacteria** break down the waste in the water. Then the water flows out of pipes into an area of soil and rocks called a drainfield.

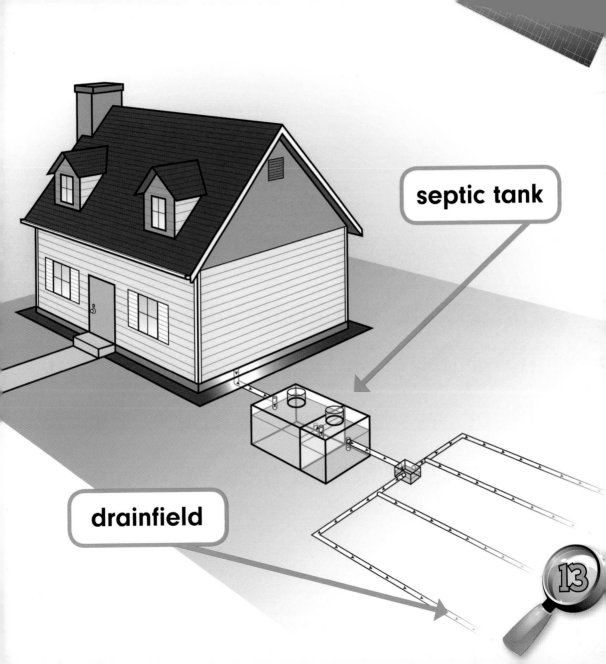

septic tank

drainfield

13

What's a Sewer System?

In some places, wastewater leaves homes and enters a sewer system. The drains in a home all lead to the same pipe. The pipes from all the homes on a street empty into a larger pipe called a sewer main.

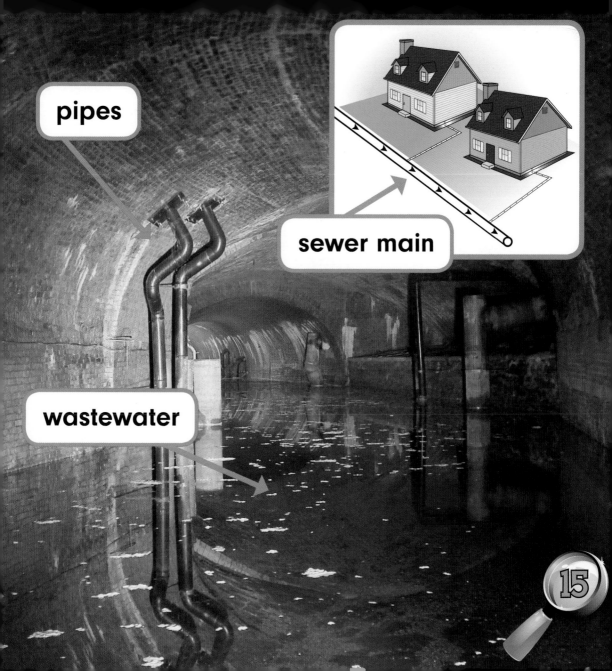

pipes

sewer main

wastewater

15

Water Treatment

Sewer water flows through the sewer main to a **treatment** plant. There, the wastewater goes through several steps to clean it. Solid waste is separated from the wastewater. Bacteria and **chemicals** are used to clean the wastewater.

After Treatment

The water from treatment plants isn't clean enough to use in homes. Most of it is mixed into large bodies of water to make it safe again. However, some is used to water crops, parks, and golf courses.

Keep Our Water Safe

Everyone needs water to live. We need to help **conserve** water and keep it clean and safe. Never dump harmful chemicals into public water supplies. Save water by collecting rainwater for your plants instead of using tap water.

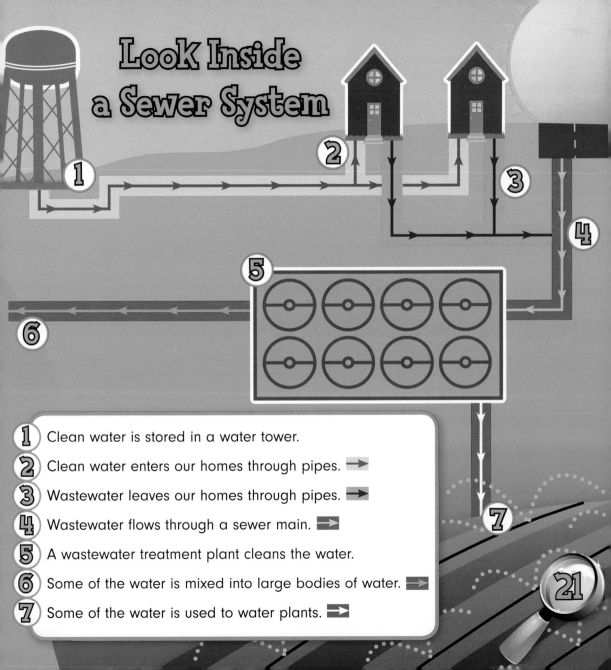

Look Inside a Sewer System

1. Clean water is stored in a water tower.
2. Clean water enters our homes through pipes.
3. Wastewater leaves our homes through pipes.
4. Wastewater flows through a sewer main.
5. A wastewater treatment plant cleans the water.
6. Some of the water is mixed into large bodies of water.
7. Some of the water is used to water plants.

21

Glossary

bacteria: tiny creatures that can only be seen with a microscope

chemical: matter that can be mixed with other matter to cause changes

conserve: to keep something from harm and not waste it

drain: a pipe that carries water away from a place

gravity: the force that pulls objects towards Earth's center

tank: a large container for storing things

treatment: steps used to change or improve something

For More Information

Books

Horn, Geoffrey M. *Sewer Inspector*. New York, NY: Marshall Cavendish Benchmark, 2010.

Oxlade, Chris, and Anita Ganeri. *Down the Drain: Conserving Water*. Chicago, IL: Heinemann Library, 2005.

Websites

Wastewater—Sewage in Your Face
www.sandiego.gov/mwwd/kids
Learn more about sewer systems and wastewater treatment by reading articles, watching videos, and playing games.

Water—Use It Wisely
www.wateruseitwisely.com/kids
Learn more about how to conserve water.

Index

APPRENTIS LECTEURS

PIEDS EN L'AIR, PIEDS SUR TERRE

Pamela Love

Illustrations de Lynne Chapman

Texte français d'Ann Lamontagne

Éditions
■SCHOLASTIC

À mes grands-parents,
Russell et Agnes Cushman et Ray et Meta Gibson
— P.L.

Pour Talia et Melissa
— L.C.

Catalogage avant publication de Bibliothèque
et Archives Canada

Love, Pamela, 1966-
Pieds en l'air, pieds sur terre / Pamela Love;
illustrations de Lynne Chapman;
texte français d'Ann Lamontagne.

(Apprentis lecteurs)
Traduction de : Two feet up, two feet down.
Niveau d'intérêt selon l'âge: Pour enfants de 3 à 6 ans.
ISBN 978-0-545-99222-0

I. Lamontagne, Ann II. Chapman, Lynne, 1960-
III. Titre. IV. Collection.

PZ23.L677Pie 2008   j813'.6   C2007-906031-5

Édition publiée par les Éditions Scholastic,
604, rue King Ouest, Toronto (Ontario) M5V 1E1.

5 4 3 2 1   Imprimé au Canada   08 09 10 11 12

Pieds en l'air!

Pieds sur terre!
Fais tourner la corde à sauter
sans t'arrêter.

Saute toute seule...

8

ou avec des amis,
un à chaque bout,
une au milieu,
c'est réussi!

Fais-la bien tourner!
Fais de grands cercles!

Moi, je sors.
Qui veut entrer?

Saute à la corde
à l'intérieur.

15

Saute à la corde
à l'extérieur,

18

au terrain de jeux,
c'est mieux à deux.

Saute sur un pied,
puis sur les deux.

Sauter à la corde, c'est merveilleux!

Sauts de grenouilles,
ou de kangourous...
Sauter à la corde, c'est fou!

Prends cette corde.

Saute avec moi.

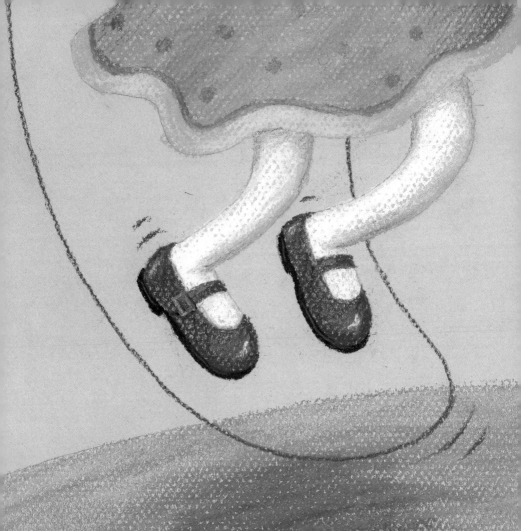

En haut, et puis en bas.

Pieds en l'air,
pieds sur terre!

LISTE DE MOTS

à	des	l'	réussi
air	deux	la	sans
amis	elle	les	saute(s)
arrêter	en	merveilleux	sauter
au	entrer	mieux	sauts
aux	est	milieu	seule
avec	et	moi	sors
bas	extérieur	ou	sur
bien	fais	pied(s)	t'
bout	fou	pour	terrain de jeux
c'	grands	prends	terre
cercles	grenouilles	près	tourne
cette	haut	puis	tourner
chaque	intérieur	qu'	toute
corde	je	qui	un(e)
de	kangourous	regarde	veut

BLUE & BERTIE

KRISTYNA LITTEN

A Paula Wiseman Book

SIMON & SCHUSTER BOOKS FOR YOUNG READERS
An imprint of Simon & Schuster Children's Publishing Division
1230 Avenue of the Americas, New York, New York 10020
Copyright © 2016 by Kristyna Litten
Originally published in Great Britain in 2016 by Simon & Schuster UK Ltd.
All rights reserved, including the right of reproduction in whole or in part in any form.

Every day Bertie and the giraffes did the same thing at the same time. *Crunchity-crunch*–they nibbled sweet leaves from the tops of the trees.

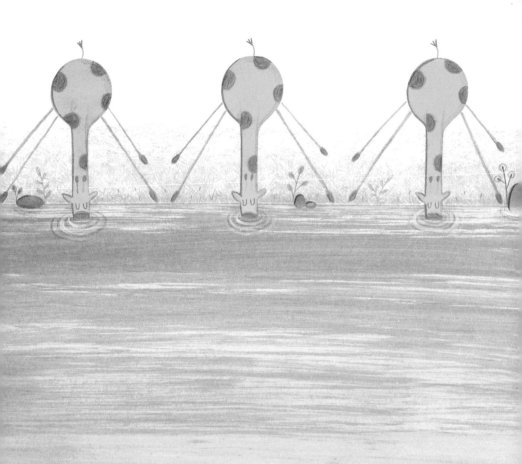

Sip, slurp–they took a cooling drink at the watering hole.

And when they were tired, they
curled their long necks, and –
snore, snore, snore –
they snoozed.

Each day was much like the last,
and that was just how they liked it.

Crunchity-crunch.
Sip, slurp.
Snore, snore, snore.

And then, one day . . .

Bertie overslept!
When he woke up,
he was alone.

Bertie was lost.

Soon big, salty tears were rolling down his cheeks.
How was Bertie going to get home?

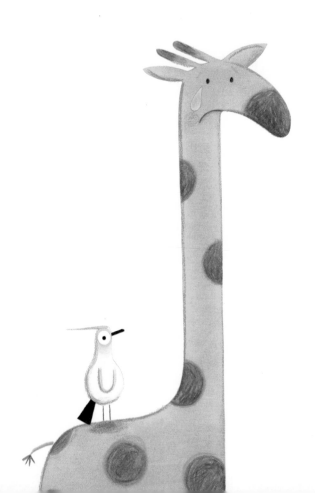

Suddenly, he heard a noise.
"Hello?" he said. "Who's there?"

"I can see you," said Bertie bravely. "And I'm not afraid."

"I am a little bit afraid of you, though," said the creature, stepping forward shyly.

Bertie was amazed.
The creature was just like him, only he was BLUE.

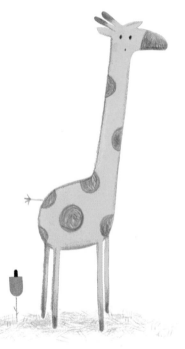

"Don't be silly," said Bertie at last.
"There's nothing to be afraid of.
I'm just a lost giraffe."

"My name is Blue," said the
creature. "I can show you
the way home if you want me to."

So – *trit trot, trit trot* – off they went together.
"You all right, there, my friend?" asked Blue.
"Very all right," said Bertie. "I never
knew all this was here!"

Gallopy-gallopy-gallopy – whoosh!
"I feel free!" cried Bertie.
"You are free, my friend," said Blue.

"I never knew there was so much to see,"
said Bertie. "Thank you, Blue."

"Why don't we do it again
tomorrow?" said Blue.
"I can't," said Bertie. "I have to *crunch,
sip,* and *snore* with all the others."

"Oh," said Blue sadly.
"Well, in that case . . .

. . . your herd is just over there."

"Yes, it is!" said Bertie.
"Hello! Hello! It's me.
I'm home, everybody!"

"Bye, Bertie," said Blue, and he turned to leave.

"Blue, wait!" called Bertie. "Aren't you coming?"

Blue hesitated.
"But I don't belong," he said.

"Trust me, my friend, you do,"
said Bertie.

Bertie was right.
The herd loved Blue, just the way he was.

From then on, the herd still *crunched* and *sipped* and *snoozed*. But now they saw things a little bit differently each day.

And that was just how they liked it.

And Blue and Bertie
remained the very best of friends.